Infrastructure Under Siege: Safeguarding Critical Systems in the 21st Century

Copyright Page

TITLE: Infrastructure Under Siege: Safeguarding Critical Systems in the 21st Century

1ST Edition

Copyright @ 2023

ISBN: 9798223004691

Table of Contents

Infrastructure Under Siege: Safeguarding Critical Systems in the 21st Century

By Roberto Miguel Rodriguez

Chapter 1: Introduction

The Importance of Critical Infrastructure Protection

In today's interconnected world, the protection of critical infrastructure has become a paramount concern. From energy facilities and communication networks to water treatment plants, these vital systems are the backbone of our society. They enable us to function and thrive, ensuring the smooth operation of various sectors such as transportation, healthcare, and finance. However, these infrastructures are increasingly vulnerable to attacks and disruptions, making the need for robust protection measures imperative.

The consequences of a successful attack on critical infrastructure can be far-reaching and devastating. Disruptions in energy supply can lead to power outages, crippling entire cities and causing significant economic losses. Communication networks are essential for timely information dissemination and emergency response coordination, making them attractive targets for cybercriminals or hostile entities seeking to disrupt communications during times of crisis. Additionally, water treatment plants are indispensable for maintaining public health, and any disruption in their functioning can have severe consequences for communities.

Protecting critical infrastructure is not just a responsibility of governments and security agencies but also of academia, the media, and other stakeholders. Professors and students play a crucial role in researching and developing innovative solutions to safeguard these systems. Their expertise can contribute to the design of resilient infrastructure that can withstand various threats, both physical and digital. Journalists have the power to raise awareness about the vulnerabilities and risks faced by critical infrastructure, encouraging public debate and holding authorities accountable for their protection.

Politicians have a duty to enact legislation and allocate resources to ensure the security and resilience of critical infrastructure. By prioritizing this issue, they can foster collaboration between public and private sectors, encouraging investment in protective measures and technology. Authors can contribute by writing books and articles that shed light on the challenges and potential solutions in this field, facilitating knowledge dissemination and encouraging critical thinking.

Security analysts and professionals specializing in infrastructure protection are crucial in identifying vulnerabilities and developing effective countermeasures. Their expertise in risk assessment, threat analysis, and incident response helps in devising strategies to prevent and mitigate potential attacks.

Ultimately, safeguarding critical infrastructure is an ongoing and collaborative effort. By recognizing its importance and engaging in proactive measures, we can ensure the resilience of these systems in the face of evolving threats. The protection of critical infrastructure is not just a matter of national security but also a safeguard for the well-being and prosperity of societies around the globe.

Defining Critical Infrastructure

In today's interconnected and technology-driven world, the protection of critical infrastructure has become paramount. From energy facilities to communication networks and water treatment plants, these vital systems underpin the functioning of our society. Understanding and defining critical infrastructure is crucial for policymakers, security analysts, and all those concerned with safeguarding these systems in the 21st century.

Critical infrastructure can be broadly defined as the physical and virtual assets that are essential for the functioning of a society and its economy. These assets include but are not limited to power plants, transportation networks, telecommunications systems, financial institutions, and healthcare facilities. They are the lifeblood of modern civilization, enabling the delivery of essential services and ensuring the smooth operation of various sectors.

One key aspect of critical infrastructure is its interdependencies. These systems are highly interconnected and rely on each other to function effectively. For instance, a disruption in the energy sector can have a cascading effect on other sectors such as transportation, communication, and healthcare. Understanding these interdependencies is crucial for assessing vulnerabilities and designing comprehensive protection strategies.

The resilience of critical infrastructure is another critical aspect that needs to be addressed. Resilience refers to the ability of these systems to withstand and recover from various threats, including physical attacks, cyber-attacks, natural disasters, and accidents. Enhancing resilience requires a multi-faceted approach, including robust security measures, redundancy, contingency plans, and effective response mechanisms.

In recent years, the threat landscape facing critical infrastructure has evolved significantly. Traditional physical threats, such as terrorist attacks, remain a concern. However, the rise of cyber threats poses a formidable challenge. Cyber-attacks can disrupt essential services, compromise sensitive data, and even lead to physical damage. Addressing these evolving threats requires a comprehensive approach that integrates physical and cybersecurity measures.

To effectively safeguard critical infrastructure, collaboration among various stakeholders is crucial. This includes government agencies, private sector entities, academia, and research institutions. Sharing information, best practices, and expertise can help identify vulnerabilities, develop innovative solutions, and enhance the overall resilience of these vital systems.

In conclusion, defining critical infrastructure is essential for understanding the interconnected systems that underpin our society. Protecting these systems from physical and cyber threats requires a comprehensive approach that considers interdependencies and resilience. Collaboration among stakeholders is crucial to effectively safeguard these critical systems and ensure their continued operation in the face of evolving challenges. By doing so, we can safeguard the foundations of our modern civilization and ensure a secure and resilient future.

The Increasing Vulnerabilities in the 21st Century

In the rapidly evolving landscape of the 21st century, our society has become increasingly dependent on critical infrastructure systems. From energy facilities to communication networks and water treatment plants, these systems play a crucial role in our daily lives. However, the advancements in technology and the interconnectedness of these systems have also made them vulnerable to a wide range of threats.

This subchapter aims to shed light on the rising vulnerabilities that our critical infrastructure faces in the modern era. By examining the challenges posed by both physical and cyber threats, we can better understand the need for robust protective measures.

One of the key factors contributing to the vulnerabilities of our critical infrastructure is the rapid pace of technological advancements. While these advancements have undoubtedly brought numerous benefits, they have also opened up new avenues for malicious actors to exploit. Cyberattacks targeting energy grids, communication networks, and other vital systems have become increasingly sophisticated and frequent. As a result, the potential for widespread disruption and chaos looms larger than ever before.

Furthermore, the increasing interconnectivity of these systems has created a domino effect, wherein a single vulnerability can have far-reaching consequences. An attack on one critical infrastructure system can easily cascade into a broader disruption, impacting multiple sectors and compromising the overall functioning of society.

Additionally, the physical vulnerabilities of critical infrastructure cannot be overlooked. The aging infrastructure in many regions, combined with the lack of adequate protective measures, poses a significant risk. Natural disasters, accidents, and physical attacks can cause severe damage to these systems, leading to prolonged disruptions and potential loss of life.

To address these vulnerabilities, a multifaceted approach is required. This includes investing in research and development to enhance the resilience of critical infrastructure systems, as well as developing robust security protocols to defend against cyber threats. Collaboration among various stakeholders, including government agencies, private sector entities, and academia, is crucial to ensure a comprehensive and effective response.

Furthermore, raising awareness among the general public about the importance of safeguarding critical infrastructure is vital. By understanding the potential consequences of system failures, individuals can contribute to a culture of security and resilience.

In conclusion, the increasing vulnerabilities faced by critical infrastructure systems in the 21st century demand immediate attention and proactive measures. This subchapter serves as a call to action for professors, students, journalists, politicians, authors, and security analysts to recognize the urgency of the situation and work together to safeguard our critical systems. Only through collective efforts can we ensure the resilience and continuity of our vital infrastructure in the face of evolving threats.

Chapter 2: Understanding Infrastructure Vulnerabilities

Historical Attacks on Critical Infrastructure

Critical infrastructure plays a vital role in the functioning of modern societies, providing essential services such as energy, communication, and water supply. However, throughout history, these critical systems have been targeted by various forms of attacks, posing significant threats to national security and public safety. This subchapter explores the historical attacks on critical infrastructure, highlighting the importance of safeguarding these systems in the 21st century.

The evolution of attacks on critical infrastructure can be traced back to both conventional warfare and acts of terrorism. During World War II, strategic bombing campaigns targeted key infrastructure, aiming to disrupt supply chains and cripple enemy capabilities. The destruction of bridges, railroads, and power plants had a profound impact on the ability to sustain both military operations and civilian life.

In recent decades, the threat landscape has expanded to include cyberattacks on critical infrastructure. As societies have become increasingly reliant on computerized systems, malicious actors have found new avenues to exploit vulnerabilities. Stuxnet, a sophisticated computer worm, famously targeted Iran's nuclear facilities in 2010, causing physical damage to centrifuges and setting a precedent for future cyber-physical attacks.

Additionally, acts of terrorism have taken aim at critical infrastructure to instill fear, disrupt services, and gain attention. The attacks on the World Trade Center in 2001 demonstrated the vulnerability of iconic structures and the potential for catastrophic consequences. More recently, attacks on power grids, communication networks, and transportation systems have highlighted the need for comprehensive protection of critical infrastructure.

To safeguard critical systems in the 21st century, it is essential to adopt a multidimensional approach. This includes technological advancements such as intrusion detection systems, firewalls, and encryption to secure digital networks. Physical security measures, such as access controls, surveillance systems, and perimeter protection, must also be implemented to prevent unauthorized access to critical infrastructure sites.

Moreover, collaboration between government agencies, private sector entities, and academia is crucial for sharing threat intelligence, conducting risk assessments, and developing robust response plans. By fostering partnerships and information-sharing initiatives, vulnerabilities can be identified and addressed before they are exploited.

In conclusion, the historical attacks on critical infrastructure serve as a stark reminder of the vulnerabilities that exist in our modern societies. As technology continues to advance, the risks associated with these attacks evolve as well. Protecting critical infrastructure requires a comprehensive and collaborative approach that encompasses both physical and digital security measures. By safeguarding our critical systems, we can ensure the resilience and reliability of essential services, contributing to the overall security and well-being of nations and their citizens.

Modern Threats and Risks

In this subchapter, we delve into the pressing issue of modern threats and risks that pose significant challenges to safeguarding critical infrastructure in the 21st century. As the world becomes increasingly interconnected and dependent on complex systems, it is crucial to understand and address these threats to ensure the resilience of our vital infrastructure.

The rapid advancement of technology has brought numerous benefits, but it has also opened the door to new vulnerabilities. Cyberattacks, for instance, have emerged as a major concern, with hackers targeting energy facilities, communication networks, and water treatment plants. These attacks can disrupt essential services, compromise sensitive information, and even threaten public safety. As professors, students, journalists, politicians, authors, and security analysts, it is essential for us to comprehend the gravity of these threats and work towards effective solutions.

The increasing reliance on interconnected systems, commonly referred to as the Internet of Things (IoT), presents another significant risk. With billions of devices connected to the internet, including critical infrastructure components, the potential for exploitation grows exponentially. As security analysts, it is imperative for us to understand the vulnerabilities inherent in these systems and devise strategies to protect against cyber threats.

Furthermore, the rise of state-sponsored attacks adds a new dimension to the modern threat landscape. Governments and political actors are increasingly using cyber tactics to target critical infrastructure and disrupt the operations of rival nations. This has far-reaching implications for national security and requires a comprehensive approach to ensure the resilience of our essential services.

Addressing these modern threats and risks requires collaboration and interdisciplinary efforts. Professors can contribute by developing educational programs that equip students with the necessary skills to protect critical infrastructure. Journalists can raise public awareness about these issues, holding politicians accountable for implementing robust security measures. Authors can write compelling narratives that highlight the potential consequences of neglecting infrastructure protection. Meanwhile, security analysts can continuously assess and evaluate emerging threats, providing valuable insights to policymakers.

In conclusion, the challenges posed by modern threats and risks to critical infrastructure demand immediate attention. As a diverse audience consisting of professors, students, journalists, politicians, authors, and security analysts, we must collectively work towards safeguarding our vital systems. By understanding the nature of these threats and collaborating on effective solutions, we can ensure the resilience and security of our critical infrastructure in the 21st century and beyond.

Cybersecurity Challenges for Critical Systems

Subchapter: Cybersecurity Challenges for Critical Systems

In today's interconnected world, the protection of critical infrastructure has become a paramount concern for governments, organizations, and individuals alike. As our societies become more reliant on technology, the vulnerabilities of our critical systems are increasingly exposed to a wide range of cyber threats. This subchapter delves into the pressing issue of cybersecurity challenges faced by critical systems and explores the measures that need to be taken to ensure their resilience against attacks and disruptions.

The digitization of critical infrastructure, including energy facilities, communication networks, and water treatment plants, has brought numerous benefits in terms of efficiency, automation, and improved services. However, this digital transformation has also opened up vulnerabilities that can be exploited by malicious actors. The increasing complexity and interconnectedness of critical systems make them attractive targets for cybercriminals, hacktivists, terrorists, and even nation-states seeking to disrupt essential services, cause economic damage, or compromise national security.

One of the primary cybersecurity challenges for critical systems is the constantly evolving nature of cyber threats. Traditional security measures are no longer sufficient to combat the sophisticated tactics employed by cybercriminals. Attack vectors such as ransomware, distributed denial-of-service (DDoS) attacks, and advanced persistent threats (APTs) pose significant risks to the availability, integrity, and confidentiality of critical systems. Moreover, the interconnectedness of these systems means that a successful attack on one component can have cascading effects on others, amplifying the potential damage.

To address these challenges, a multi-faceted approach is required. First and foremost, robust cybersecurity frameworks and standards must be developed and implemented across all critical infrastructure sectors. These frameworks should encompass risk assessment, threat intelligence, incident response, and continuous monitoring to detect and mitigate cyber threats promptly.

Education and awareness are also vital components of safeguarding critical systems. Professors, students, and security analysts play a pivotal role in raising awareness about the potential consequences of cyber attacks on critical infrastructure. By studying and researching these challenges, they can contribute to the development of innovative solutions and best practices that can be shared with policymakers, politicians, and industry professionals.

Collaboration and information sharing among stakeholders are crucial in the fight against cyber threats. Governments, organizations, and experts must work together to exchange threat intelligence, share best practices, and coordinate response efforts. This collaboration should extend beyond national borders to address the global nature of cyber threats.

In conclusion, the cybersecurity challenges faced by critical systems in the 21st century are significant and require urgent attention. By acknowledging the evolving nature of cyber threats, implementing robust security measures, raising awareness, and fostering collaboration, we can improve the resilience of our critical infrastructure and safeguard the essential services upon which our societies depend. It is a collective responsibility that requires the active participation of professors, students, journalists, politicians, authors, security analysts, and all stakeholders involved in the protection of critical infrastructure.

Chapter 3: Energy Facilities Protection

Securing Power Plants and Electrical Grids

In an increasingly interconnected world, the security of power plants and electrical grids has become a paramount concern for governments, industries, and individuals alike. As our reliance on electricity continues to grow exponentially, so does the potential for catastrophic disruptions caused by intentional attacks or natural disasters. In this subchapter, we delve into the critical importance of safeguarding these vital infrastructures and explore the strategies and technologies employed to ensure their resilience in the face of evolving threats.

Power plants and electrical grids represent the backbone of modern society, enabling everything from transportation and communication to healthcare and commerce. The consequences of a successful attack on these systems can be devastating, leading to widespread power outages, economic disruption, and even loss of life. It is imperative that we adopt a proactive approach to anticipate and mitigate risks, and this chapter aims to shed light on the various measures taken to achieve this.

One key aspect of securing power plants and electrical grids is enhancing physical security. This involves implementing stringent access control measures, such as biometric authentication and surveillance systems, to prevent unauthorized individuals from gaining entry to critical facilities. Additionally, the deployment of advanced perimeter security technologies, such as intrusion detection systems and video analytics, can detect and deter potential threats before they reach vulnerable targets.

However, physical security alone is not enough to safeguard these complex systems. Cybersecurity has emerged as an equally significant aspect, given the increasing reliance on digital control systems and interconnected networks. Hackers and other malicious actors pose a significant threat to the integrity and functionality of power plants and electrical grids. Robust cybersecurity measures, including regular vulnerability assessments, network monitoring, and the implementation of encryption protocols, are vital to protect against cyber threats and maintain the integrity of critical energy infrastructure.

To ensure the resilience of power plants and electrical grids, industry professionals, government agencies, and academia must collaborate closely. Research and development initiatives aimed at identifying vulnerabilities and developing innovative security solutions are crucial. Furthermore, training programs should be established to equip personnel with the necessary skills and knowledge to detect and respond to potential threats effectively.

In conclusion, securing power plants and electrical grids is a multifaceted challenge that requires a comprehensive approach. By combining physical security measures with robust cybersecurity protocols and fostering collaboration among various stakeholders, we can ensure the resilience of these critical infrastructures. The protection of power plants and electrical grids is not only essential for the smooth functioning of our societies but is also vital for maintaining national security and economic stability in the 21st century.

Challenges and Solutions in Nuclear Power Plants

Introduction:

In the contemporary world, nuclear power plants play a crucial role in meeting the energy demands of nations. However, these critical systems face numerous challenges that need to be addressed to ensure their resilience against attacks and disruptions. This subchapter aims to explore the challenges faced by nuclear power plants and propose potential solutions to mitigate them.

Challenges:

1. Safety and Security Concerns:

Nuclear power plants are exposed to various safety and security risks, including natural disasters, technical failures, and terrorist attacks. Ensuring the safety of personnel and the public, as well as safeguarding nuclear materials, remains a primary challenge.

2. Aging Infrastructure:

Many nuclear power plants were built several decades ago and are now facing aging infrastructure issues. The degradation of critical components and systems poses potential risks to their safe and efficient operation.

3. Public Perception and Acceptance:

Public perception of nuclear power plants is often influenced by concerns over the long-term storage of nuclear waste and the potential for accidents. Overcoming public skepticism and fostering acceptance is crucial for the continued development and operation of nuclear power plants.

Solutions:

1. Enhanced Safety and Security Measures:

Implementing robust safety and security measures is imperative to safeguard nuclear power plants. This includes investing in advanced technologies for early detection and prevention of accidents, developing stringent security protocols, and ensuring the availability of skilled personnel to respond to emergencies promptly.

2. Upgrading and Modernizing Infrastructure:

Investing in the upgrading and modernization of aging infrastructure is essential to ensure the continued safe and efficient operation of nuclear power plants. This includes the replacement of critical components, such as reactor vessels and containment structures, as well as the implementation of advanced monitoring and maintenance systems.

3. Transparency and Public Engagement:

Nuclear power plants should focus on enhancing transparency and engaging with the public to address concerns and misconceptions. This can be achieved through educational programs, public consultations, and open dialogue with stakeholders, fostering trust and acceptance of nuclear power as a viable and sustainable energy source.

Conclusion:

Nuclear power plants face various challenges that need to be effectively addressed to ensure their resilience and continued contribution to meeting energy demands. By implementing enhanced safety and security measures, upgrading aging infrastructure, and fostering transparency and public engagement, nuclear power plants can strive towards a more secure and sustainable energy future. It is imperative for professors, students, journalists, politicians, authors, and security analysts to understand and contribute to the discourse surrounding the challenges and solutions in nuclear power plants, as it directly impacts the critical infrastructure protection and resilience of nations.

Renewable Energy Infrastructure Protection

In recent years, the global shift towards renewable energy sources has been gaining momentum, driven by concerns over climate change and the need for sustainable development. As countries strive to reduce their carbon footprint and secure a clean energy future, the construction and maintenance of renewable energy infrastructure have become critical factors. However, with the increasing reliance on these systems, the need to protect them from potential threats and disruptions has become equally important.

The subchapter "Renewable Energy Infrastructure Protection" focuses on the challenges and strategies involved in safeguarding critical renewable energy facilities. Addressing a diverse audience of professors, students, journalists, politicians, authors, and security analysts, this chapter aims to raise awareness about the vulnerabilities of renewable energy infrastructure and the significance of protecting them.

The chapter begins by highlighting the critical role of renewable energy infrastructure in ensuring a sustainable and reliable energy supply. It emphasizes the interconnectedness of energy facilities, communication networks, and water treatment plants, and the potential cascading effects of disruptions or attacks on these interconnected systems. By showcasing real-world examples of previous incidents and their consequences, the chapter underscores the urgency of investing in infrastructure protection.

Next, the subchapter delves into the specific threats faced by renewable energy installations. It explores traditional physical threats such as vandalism, theft, and sabotage, as well as emerging cyber threats that can compromise the integrity and functionality of these systems. Drawing upon the expertise of security analysts, the chapter provides an in-depth analysis of potential vulnerabilities and their implications for energy security.

To address these challenges, the chapter proposes a comprehensive framework for renewable energy infrastructure protection. It discusses the importance of collaboration between governments, energy providers, and security agencies in developing resilience strategies. The chapter also explores the role of advanced technologies, such as surveillance systems, intrusion detection systems, and artificial intelligence, in fortifying the security of renewable energy infrastructure.

Furthermore, the subchapter examines the legal and regulatory aspects of infrastructure protection, highlighting the need for updated policies and legislation to effectively address emerging threats and ensure compliance. It also emphasizes the importance of public awareness and education in fostering a culture of security consciousness.

In conclusion, "Renewable Energy Infrastructure Protection" sheds light on the critical need to safeguard renewable energy facilities. By presenting a comprehensive overview of the challenges, strategies, and technologies involved in protecting these critical systems, this subchapter aims to empower professors, students, journalists, politicians, authors, and security analysts with the knowledge necessary to contribute to the resilience and security of renewable energy infrastructure in the 21st century.

Chapter 4: Communication Networks Resilience

Safeguarding Telecommunication Infrastructure

In today's interconnected world, telecommunication infrastructure plays a crucial role in facilitating communication, commerce, and innovation. From the internet to mobile networks, these systems have become the backbone of our modern society. However, as our reliance on these technologies grows, so does the need to safeguard them from potential threats and disruptions.

The subchapter "Safeguarding Telecommunication Infrastructure" delves into the critical importance of protecting these systems and ensuring their resilience against attacks and disruptions. Addressed to professors, students, journalists, politicians, authors, and security analysts, this subchapter aims to provide a comprehensive understanding of the challenges and strategies involved in protecting this vital infrastructure.

The subchapter begins by highlighting the increasing dependence on telecommunication infrastructure and the potential consequences of its failure. It explores the interconnectedness of various sectors, such as energy facilities, communication networks, and water treatment plants, emphasizing the need for a holistic approach to infrastructure protection.

Next, the subchapter delves into the various threats faced by telecommunication infrastructure. These can range from physical attacks, such as sabotage and vandalism, to cyber threats, including hacking, data breaches, and malware attacks. It explores real-world examples of past incidents to illustrate the potential consequences and the urgency of safeguarding these systems.

To address these threats, the subchapter discusses various strategies and best practices for safeguarding telecommunication infrastructure. It explores the importance of risk assessment and the need for proactive measures in identifying vulnerabilities. It also delves into the role of technology in enhancing security, such as advanced encryption, intrusion detection systems, and secure protocols.

Furthermore, the subchapter emphasizes the need for collaboration between public and private entities, as well as international cooperation, in protecting telecommunication infrastructure. It explores the role of legislation, regulations, and standards in ensuring the resilience of these systems. It also highlights the importance of public awareness and education in fostering a culture of security.

Overall, "Safeguarding Telecommunication Infrastructure" provides a comprehensive overview of the challenges and strategies involved in protecting this critical system. It aims to equip professors, students, journalists, politicians, authors, and security analysts with the knowledge and understanding necessary to contribute to the ongoing efforts in infrastructure protection. By highlighting the importance of resilience and collaboration, this subchapter underscores the urgent need to safeguard telecommunication infrastructure in the 21st century.

Cybersecurity Risks to Communication Networks

In today's interconnected world, communication networks play a vital role in facilitating the flow of information and enabling seamless connectivity. However, as our reliance on these networks grows, so does the potential for cyber threats and attacks. This subchapter aims to shed light on the various cybersecurity risks faced by communication networks, exploring the challenges and potential solutions in safeguarding these critical systems.

The rapid advancements in technology have paved the way for increased connectivity and efficiency. However, they have also created vulnerabilities that malicious actors can exploit. Communication networks, including the internet, mobile networks, and satellite systems, are not immune to these risks. From state-sponsored attacks to criminal activities, the threats to communication networks are diverse and constantly evolving.

One of the primary concerns is the potential disruption of communication services. A successful cyber attack could compromise the availability and reliability of these networks, leading to significant disruptions in various sectors such as finance, healthcare, transportation, and government services. Such disruptions could have far-reaching consequences, affecting not only individuals but also the overall economy and national security.

Another critical aspect is the protection of sensitive data transmitted through these networks. Communication networks are the backbone of information exchange, making them attractive targets for data breaches and espionage. Unauthorized access to sensitive information, such as personal data, trade secrets, or classified government intelligence, can have severe implications for individuals, businesses, and national security.

Addressing these risks requires a multi-faceted approach. Robust cybersecurity measures, including encryption, firewalls, intrusion detection systems, and regular security audits, are essential in fortifying communication networks against potential threats. Additionally, collaboration and information sharing among stakeholders, including governments, service providers, and security experts, are crucial in staying ahead of emerging threats.

Education and awareness are also key components in mitigating cybersecurity risks. Professors, students, journalists, politicians, authors, and security analysts must be well-informed about the challenges and potential solutions surrounding communication network security. By fostering a culture of cybersecurity and promoting best practices, we can empower individuals and organizations to recognize and address potential risks effectively.

In conclusion, the cybersecurity risks to communication networks are a pressing concern in the 21st century. As our reliance on these critical systems grows, so does the need for robust protection against potential threats. By understanding the challenges, implementing effective security measures, and fostering awareness, we can safeguard our communication networks and ensure their resilience against attacks and disruptions.

Protecting Data Centers and Internet Exchange Points

In the digital age, data centers and internet exchange points (IXPs) serve as the backbone of our interconnected world. These critical infrastructures not only store vast amounts of valuable information but also facilitate the exchange of data that powers our daily lives. However, the increasing reliance on technology and the growing threat landscape have made data centers and IXPs prime targets for malicious actors seeking to disrupt vital services and compromise sensitive data.

The protection of data centers and IXPs is of utmost importance in ensuring the resilience of our critical infrastructure. This subchapter explores the various security measures and best practices that must be implemented to safeguard these essential facilities.

Physical security forms the foundation of protecting data centers and IXPs. Access control systems, surveillance cameras, and perimeter fencing are crucial components in restricting unauthorized entry and deterring potential threats. Additionally, the implementation of robust physical security measures such as biometric authentication and mantraps can further fortify these facilities against unauthorized access attempts.

However, physical security alone is not sufficient to protect against the sophisticated cyber threats faced by data centers and IXPs. Robust cybersecurity measures must also be employed to defend against malicious activities such as distributed denial-of-service (DDoS) attacks, data breaches, and malware infections. This includes deploying firewalls, intrusion detection and prevention systems, and robust encryption protocols to safeguard data in transit and at rest.

Moreover, continuous monitoring and threat intelligence gathering are vital in identifying and mitigating potential security vulnerabilities. Implementing security information and event management (SIEM) systems, conducting regular penetration testing, and engaging in threat intelligence sharing are essential practices to stay one step ahead of evolving threats.

Collaboration between industry stakeholders, government bodies, and security analysts is crucial in protecting data centers and IXPs effectively. Regular audits and compliance assessments can enforce security standards and ensure the implementation of best practices. Additionally, public-private partnerships can foster knowledge sharing and cooperation in developing innovative security solutions.

As technology advances, the protection of data centers and IXPs must evolve to match the sophistication of emerging threats. By implementing stringent physical security measures, robust cybersecurity protocols, and fostering collaboration among stakeholders, we can safeguard these critical infrastructures and ensure their resilience against attacks and disruptions. Only through a comprehensive and proactive approach can we secure the foundation of our interconnected world and protect the valuable data that underpins modern society.

Chapter 5: Water Treatment Plants Security

Ensuring Safe and Secure Water Supply

In today's interconnected world, the protection of critical infrastructure is of paramount importance. One such vital component is the water supply, which plays a fundamental role in sustaining life and maintaining societal functions. This subchapter aims to shed light on the challenges and strategies involved in safeguarding our water treatment plants and ensuring a safe and secure water supply for all.

Water treatment plants are part of our critical infrastructure, and their resilience against potential attacks and disruptions is a pressing concern. These facilities face numerous threats, ranging from physical attacks to cyber-attacks, which can severely impact the continuity of water supply and compromise public health and safety. As such, a comprehensive approach to infrastructure protection is necessary to address these risks effectively.

Physical security measures are essential in safeguarding water treatment plants. Perimeter fencing, access control systems, surveillance cameras, and security personnel are some of the key components of a robust physical security plan. Regular security audits and vulnerability assessments should be conducted to identify potential weaknesses and implement remedial measures promptly.

However, in today's digital age, cyber threats pose an equally significant risk to water supply systems. Water treatment plants are increasingly connected to computer networks, making them vulnerable to cyber-attacks that can disrupt operations and compromise the integrity of the water supply. Therefore, a robust cybersecurity framework is essential to protect these critical systems. This includes implementing firewalls, intrusion detection systems, encryption protocols, and regular software updates to mitigate vulnerabilities.

Collaboration and information sharing among stakeholders are crucial in ensuring the safety and security of our water supply. Professors, students, journalists, politicians, authors, and security analysts all have a role to play in raising awareness about the importance of protecting our critical infrastructure. By fostering interdisciplinary research, developing policies, and promoting best practices, we can work together to enhance the resilience of our water treatment plants.

Furthermore, policymakers must allocate adequate resources to support infrastructure protection initiatives. This includes investing in state-of-the-art technologies, providing training and education programs, and establishing regulatory frameworks that enforce security standards across the water industry.

In conclusion, safeguarding our water supply is a collective responsibility that requires the collaboration of various stakeholders. By implementing robust physical security measures, establishing a comprehensive cybersecurity framework, and fostering collaboration and information sharing, we can ensure a safe and secure water supply for present and future generations. It is imperative that professors, students, journalists, politicians, authors, and security analysts all play an active role in addressing the challenges faced by water treatment plants and advocating for the protection of critical infrastructure. Together, we can build a resilient and sustainable future.

Vulnerabilities and Threats to Water Treatment Plants

In today's interconnected world, where technology plays a crucial role in various sectors, safeguarding critical infrastructure, including water treatment plants, is of utmost importance. Water treatment plants are vital to our daily lives, ensuring the supply of clean and safe drinking water to millions of people. However, these facilities are not immune to vulnerabilities and threats that could potentially disrupt their operations and jeopardize public health.

One of the primary vulnerabilities faced by water treatment plants is physical security. These facilities often span large areas and are equipped with complex machinery, making them challenging to secure adequately. Intruders or unauthorized individuals gaining access to these premises can tamper with the equipment, contaminate the water supply, or cause significant damage, leading to widespread consequences.

Moreover, cyber threats pose another major concern for water treatment plants. With the integration of digital systems and the use of supervisory control and data acquisition (SCADA) systems, these plants are vulnerable to cyber-attacks. Malicious actors can exploit vulnerabilities in these systems, gaining unauthorized control over critical processes, manipulating water quality parameters, or even causing catastrophic failures.

The consequences of successful attacks on water treatment plants can be severe. Contaminated water supplies can result in outbreaks of waterborne diseases, affecting public health on a large scale. Moreover, the economic impact of such incidents can be significant, as the cost of remediation, public health interventions, and damage repairs can be astronomical.

Addressing these vulnerabilities and threats requires a multi-faceted approach. Water treatment plant operators must prioritize physical security measures, such as perimeter fencing, access controls, and surveillance systems, to deter unauthorized access. Regular risk assessments and vulnerability testing should be conducted to identify and rectify any weaknesses in the infrastructure.

Cybersecurity measures are equally critical in safeguarding water treatment plants. Implementing robust firewalls, intrusion detection systems, and encryption protocols can help protect SCADA systems from unauthorized access and prevent cyber-attacks. Regular security updates and patch management should be prioritized to address newly identified vulnerabilities promptly.

Collaboration between water treatment plant operators, government agencies, and security analysts is essential in developing comprehensive security strategies. Sharing best practices, threat intelligence, and conducting joint exercises can enhance the resilience of these critical facilities against potential threats.

In conclusion, water treatment plants are susceptible to vulnerabilities and threats that can disrupt their operations and compromise public health. Recognizing the significance of these challenges and implementing robust security measures is vital to ensure the resilience of these critical systems. By addressing physical security concerns, bolstering cybersecurity measures, and fostering collaboration, we can safeguard our water treatment plants and protect the well-being of our communities in the 21st century.

Emergency Response and Recovery Strategies

In an increasingly interconnected world, the protection of critical infrastructure has become a paramount concern for governments, organizations, and individuals alike. Safeguarding vital systems such as energy facilities, communication networks, and water treatment plants is essential to ensure their resilience against attacks and disruptions. This subchapter delves into the importance of emergency response and recovery strategies in the face of infrastructure threats and explores effective measures to mitigate potential damages.

Understanding the urgency and gravity of infrastructure attacks, it is crucial to establish comprehensive emergency response plans. These plans should be developed in collaboration with relevant stakeholders, including government agencies, private sector actors, and local communities. By involving a diverse range of expertise, emergency response strategies can be tailored to address specific vulnerabilities and challenges in different sectors of critical infrastructure.

A key aspect of emergency response is the establishment of effective communication networks. Timely and accurate information dissemination is essential during crisis situations, enabling swift decision-making and coordination of resources. Governments and organizations must invest in robust communication infrastructure and protocols to ensure seamless information flow between all stakeholders involved in emergency response efforts.

Moreover, recovery strategies play a crucial role in restoring normalcy after an infrastructure attack. These strategies should focus not only on physical repairs but also on the psychological and socio-economic impacts inflicted on affected communities. By addressing the immediate needs of affected individuals and businesses, recovery efforts can help rebuild trust and resilience in the aftermath of an attack.

To enhance emergency response and recovery strategies, continuous research and development are imperative. Professors, students, and security analysts have a pivotal role to play in studying past incidents, analyzing emerging threats, and developing innovative solutions. Through interdisciplinary collaboration and knowledge-sharing, we can refine existing strategies and devise new approaches to combat evolving challenges to critical infrastructure.

Journalists and authors also have a significant responsibility in raising awareness about infrastructure protection and the importance of emergency response and recovery. By reporting on successful strategies, analyzing their strengths and weaknesses, and showcasing real-life examples, they can inform the public and hold policymakers accountable for ensuring the resilience of critical systems.

Politicians, on the other hand, have the power to influence policy and allocate resources towards infrastructure protection. By prioritizing emergency response and recovery strategies in their agendas, they can foster an environment that emphasizes resilience and preparedness against potential threats.

In conclusion, the subchapter on emergency response and recovery strategies highlights the crucial role these measures play in safeguarding critical infrastructure. Addressing an audience including professors, students, journalists, politicians, authors, and security analysts, it emphasizes the need for interdisciplinary collaboration, effective communication networks, and continuous research. By harnessing collective expertise and investing in resilience, we can ensure the safety and longevity of our critical systems in the 21st century and beyond.

Chapter 6: Transportation Infrastructure Protection

Securing Transportation Networks

In today's interconnected world, transportation networks play a vital role in the functioning of our societies. Whether it is the movement of people, goods, or services, the seamless operation of transportation systems is critical for the economic prosperity and social well-being of a nation. However, with the increasing threat of terrorism, cyber attacks, and natural disasters, securing transportation networks has become a paramount concern.

This subchapter aims to shed light on the challenges faced in safeguarding transportation networks and the strategies that can be adopted to enhance their resilience. It is intended for professors, students, journalists, politicians, authors, and security analysts who are interested in infrastructure protection and ensuring the continuity of critical systems in the 21st century.

Transportation networks encompass a wide range of infrastructure, including airports, seaports, railways, highways, and public transportation systems. These networks are vulnerable to a variety of threats, such as terrorist attacks on transportation hubs, cyber attacks on control systems, and extreme weather events that can disrupt the flow of goods and people. Understanding these vulnerabilities is essential to developing effective security measures.

One of the key strategies for securing transportation networks is the implementation of robust physical security measures. This includes the deployment of surveillance cameras, access control systems, and perimeter fencing to deter potential threats. Additionally, the use of advanced screening technologies, such as explosive detection systems, can help prevent the smuggling of dangerous materials.

In the digital age, securing transportation networks also requires a strong focus on cybersecurity. The reliance on computer systems and networked technologies makes transportation networks susceptible to cyber attacks that can disrupt operations or compromise safety. Implementing robust cybersecurity protocols, including firewalls, intrusion detection systems, and regular vulnerability assessments, can mitigate these risks.

Furthermore, collaboration and information sharing among stakeholders are crucial for securing transportation networks. Governments, transportation authorities, law enforcement agencies, and private sector entities must work together to identify and address vulnerabilities. This can be achieved through the establishment of public-private partnerships, sharing of threat intelligence, and conducting joint training exercises.

In conclusion, securing transportation networks is essential to safeguard critical infrastructure and ensure their resilience against attacks and disruptions. This subchapter has provided an overview of the challenges faced in securing transportation networks and the strategies that can be adopted to enhance their security. By understanding these issues and implementing proactive measures, we can ensure the safe and efficient movement of people and goods, even in the face of evolving threats.

Airport Security and Air Traffic Control Systems

Introduction:

In today's interconnected world, the security and efficient functioning of airports and air traffic control systems are of paramount importance. These critical infrastructures play a vital role in ensuring the safe and uninterrupted movement of people and goods across the globe. However, they also face numerous challenges and vulnerabilities that need to be addressed to safeguard against potential threats and disruptions. This subchapter delves into the intricacies of airport security and air traffic control systems, highlighting their significance and exploring strategies to enhance their resilience.

The Significance of Airport Security:

Airport security serves as the first line of defense against potential threats to aviation. With the ever-evolving nature of terrorism and criminal activities, it is crucial to adopt comprehensive security measures to prevent unauthorized access, detect prohibited items, and mitigate potential risks. This subchapter discusses the various layers of airport security, encompassing passenger screening, baggage checks, employee vetting, and the use of advanced technologies to enhance overall security efficacy.

Air Traffic Control Systems and Ensuring Safety:

Air traffic control systems are the backbone of aviation, responsible for managing the flow of aircraft in the sky and on the ground. They ensure safe and efficient operations by coordinating aircraft movements, providing weather information, and managing airspace congestion. This subchapter explores the challenges faced by air traffic control systems, such as airspace capacity constraints, technological advancements, and potential cyber threats. It also highlights the need for continuous investment in infrastructure, training, and research to enhance the safety and efficiency of these systems.

Addressing Vulnerabilities and Enhancing Resilience:

To safeguard airport security and air traffic control systems, it is crucial to identify vulnerabilities and implement robust countermeasures. This subchapter discusses the importance of adopting a multi-layered approach to security, integrating intelligence gathering, risk assessment, and technology-driven solutions. It also emphasizes the need for collaborative efforts between governments, aviation authorities, and industry stakeholders to enhance information sharing and establish best practices.

Conclusion:

Airport security and air traffic control systems are critical components of our infrastructure that require continuous attention and investment. This subchapter highlights the significance of these systems and the challenges they face in the 21st century. By understanding the vulnerabilities and adopting comprehensive security measures, we can ensure the resilience of these critical infrastructures and protect the safety and efficiency of global aviation. It is essential for professors, students, journalists, politicians, authors, and security analysts to comprehend the complexities of airport security and air traffic control systems to contribute to the discourse on infrastructure protection in the 21st century.

Protecting Railways, Highways, and Ports

In an era marked by increasing connectivity and interdependence, safeguarding critical infrastructures such as railways, highways, and ports becomes paramount. The smooth functioning of these systems is essential for the economic vitality and national security of any country. "Infrastructure Under Siege: Safeguarding Critical Systems in the 21st Century" recognizes the pressing need to address the vulnerabilities faced by these vital transportation networks.

Railways serve as the lifelines of modern societies, transporting goods, people, and services across vast distances. Their disruption can have far-reaching consequences, impacting supply chains, economies, and public safety. Similarly, highways play an essential role in facilitating the movement of goods and people, enabling trade and commerce to thrive.

Ports serve as gateways to international trade, handling massive cargo volumes and ensuring the smooth flow of goods between nations.

However, these critical transportation systems face a growing range of threats, including cyberattacks, physical attacks, natural disasters, and accidents. In this subchapter, we delve into the challenges faced by railways, highways, and ports and explore strategies to protect them from such threats.

First and foremost, a comprehensive risk assessment of these infrastructure assets is imperative. Understanding the vulnerabilities and potential consequences of an attack or disruption is crucial in developing effective protective measures. This subchapter provides an overview of the risk management frameworks and methodologies used to identify and assess risks specific to railways, highways, and ports.

Additionally, technological advancements can play a pivotal role in fortifying these transportation networks. From advanced surveillance systems and intrusion detection technologies to intelligent transportation systems, the integration of cutting-edge solutions can significantly enhance security and resilience. This subchapter delves into the latest innovations and best practices in deploying technology for protection purposes.

Furthermore, collaboration and information sharing among stakeholders are vital for ensuring the security of railways, highways, and ports. This subchapter highlights successful public-private partnerships and international cooperation models that have proven effective in enhancing security and response capabilities.

Lastly, the subchapter addresses the importance of training and preparedness in protecting these critical infrastructure systems. Educating and training security personnel, first responders, and relevant stakeholders is essential for effectively mitigating risks and minimizing the impact of potential disruptions.

"Infrastructure Under Siege: Safeguarding Critical Systems in the 21st Century" aims to equip professors, students, journalists, politicians, authors, and security analysts with a comprehensive understanding of the challenges faced by railways, highways, and ports. By examining the vulnerabilities, exploring protective measures, and showcasing successful case studies, this subchapter provides a valuable resource for those interested in infrastructure protection and ensuring the resilience of critical transportation networks.

Chapter 7: Critical Infrastructure Interdependencies

Understanding Interdependencies between Critical Systems

In today's interconnected world, critical infrastructure systems play an integral role in our daily lives. From energy facilities to communication networks and water treatment plants, these systems are the backbone of our modern society. However, their very interconnectedness also makes them vulnerable to attacks and disruptions, posing significant risks to our national security and public safety.

The subchapter titled "Understanding Interdependencies between Critical Systems" delves into the complex web of interdependencies that exist between various critical infrastructure systems. It aims to provide a comprehensive understanding of how disruptions in one system can cascade and impact others, leading to potentially catastrophic consequences.

For professors, students, journalists, politicians, authors, and security analysts, this subchapter serves as an essential resource to comprehend the intricacies of infrastructure protection. By gaining insights into the interdependencies between critical systems, professionals and researchers in the field can develop informed strategies and policies to safeguard these vital components of our society.

The subchapter begins by examining the interconnections between different infrastructure systems and how they rely on each other for seamless operation. It explores scenarios where a disruption in one system, such as an attack on a power plant, can have far-reaching consequences on others, such as communication networks and water treatment plants. Through case studies and real-life examples, readers gain a deep understanding of the domino effect that can occur when critical systems fail.

Additionally, the subchapter delves into the challenges associated with identifying and understanding these interdependencies. It discusses the complexity of mapping and analyzing the vast network of connections between critical infrastructure systems, highlighting the need for advanced technological solutions and collaborative efforts.

Furthermore, the subchapter explores the importance of resilience and redundancy in mitigating the impact of interdependencies. It discusses strategies to enhance the robustness of critical systems, such as diversifying energy sources, establishing backup communication channels, and improving coordination between different sectors.

Ultimately, "Understanding Interdependencies between Critical Systems" empowers readers to comprehend the intricate nature of infrastructure protection. It equips them with the knowledge and tools necessary to develop effective strategies and policies to safeguard critical infrastructure and enhance its resilience against attacks and disruptions.

In a world where the threat landscape constantly evolves, this subchapter serves as a timely reminder of the urgent need to understand, address, and mitigate the vulnerabilities arising from interdependencies between critical systems.

Implications of Interdependencies on Infrastructure Resilience

In today's interconnected world, the resilience of critical infrastructure is of utmost importance. The increasing interdependencies among various infrastructure systems have significant implications for their ability to withstand attacks and disruptions. This subchapter delves into the implications of these interdependencies on infrastructure resilience, highlighting the challenges and potential solutions for safeguarding critical systems in the 21st century.

The complex nature of infrastructure interdependencies poses multifaceted challenges. As energy facilities, communication networks, and water treatment plants become more intertwined, a disruption in one system can have cascading effects on others. For example, a cyber-attack on a power grid could lead to a loss of communication networks and water treatment capabilities, jeopardizing public safety and welfare.

Understanding these interdependencies is crucial for developing effective strategies to safeguard critical infrastructure. Professors, students, journalists, politicians, authors, and security analysts must recognize the intricate relationships between different systems and the impact that disruptions can have on society. By studying these interdependencies, they can contribute to the development of comprehensive resilience plans and policies.

One key implication of infrastructure interdependencies is the need for collaboration among different sectors. Infrastructure protection cannot be achieved in isolation; it requires coordinated efforts from various stakeholders. Professors can educate students on the importance of interdisciplinary approaches to infrastructure resilience, while journalists can raise awareness among the general public and hold policymakers accountable. Politicians can enact legislation that promotes cooperation and information sharing, while security analysts can assess vulnerabilities and devise robust defense mechanisms.

Moreover, the interdependencies within critical infrastructure systems necessitate a holistic approach to resilience planning. Traditional siloed approaches are no longer sufficient in the face of evolving threats. Professors can emphasize the importance of systems thinking and risk assessments that consider the interdependencies among different infrastructure sectors. Students can learn to analyze the vulnerabilities and cascading effects of disruptions, enabling them to design more resilient systems. Journalists can highlight case studies that exemplify the consequences of interdependencies, fostering public understanding and support for comprehensive resilience efforts.

In conclusion, the implications of interdependencies on infrastructure resilience are far-reaching. Professors, students, journalists, politicians, authors, and security analysts all have a role to play in safeguarding critical systems against attacks and disruptions. By understanding and addressing these interdependencies, we can ensure the resilience of our infrastructure in the 21st century.

Coordinating Response and Recovery Efforts

In the face of emerging threats and increasing vulnerabilities, the ability to coordinate response and recovery efforts has become paramount in safeguarding critical infrastructure in the 21st century. This subchapter delves into the crucial role of effective coordination in ensuring the resilience of infrastructure systems against attacks and disruptions.

In today's interconnected world, where energy facilities, communication networks, and water treatment plants serve as the lifeblood of societies, any disruption can have far-reaching consequences. Coordinating response and recovery efforts is essential to minimize the impact of such disruptions and restore normalcy swiftly.

This subchapter highlights the importance of collaboration and partnership among various stakeholders in the response and recovery process. Professors, students, journalists, politicians, authors, and security analysts all play a vital role in understanding, analyzing, and disseminating information about critical infrastructure protection. By working together, these diverse groups can contribute their expertise and perspectives, leading to comprehensive and effective response strategies.

The subchapter explores the challenges faced in coordinating response and recovery efforts and offers practical solutions. It discusses the need for clear lines of communication and information sharing among stakeholders, enabling them to act swiftly and decisively in times of crisis. It emphasizes the importance of developing robust contingency plans and conducting regular drills and exercises to test the effectiveness of these plans.

Furthermore, this subchapter addresses the role of technology in enhancing coordination efforts. It examines the use of advanced communication systems, data analytics, and artificial intelligence to improve situational awareness and enable real-time decision-making. It also highlights the importance of investing in training and capacity-building initiatives to ensure that stakeholders are well-prepared to respond to emerging threats.

Lastly, this subchapter outlines the potential benefits of international cooperation in coordinating response and recovery efforts. Given that critical infrastructure is often interconnected across borders, collaboration among nations becomes crucial. It explores the importance of sharing best practices, intelligence, and resources to enhance preparedness and response capabilities globally.

In conclusion, effective coordination of response and recovery efforts is pivotal in safeguarding critical infrastructure systems. This subchapter provides valuable insights and guidance to professors, students, journalists, politicians, authors, and security analysts, emphasizing the need for collaboration, technology, and international cooperation. By working together, we can ensure the resilience of our critical systems and protect the fundamental pillars of our societies.

Chapter 8: Policy and Legal Frameworks

National and International Infrastructure Protection Policies

In today's interconnected world, safeguarding critical infrastructure has become a top priority for governments and organizations around the globe. As societies rely more and more on energy facilities, communication networks, and water treatment plants, the need to protect these vital systems from attacks and disruptions has never been more pressing. This subchapter explores the various national and international infrastructure protection policies that have been put in place to ensure the resilience of critical systems in the 21st century.

National Infrastructure Protection Policies:

Governments play a crucial role in establishing policies and frameworks to protect their national infrastructure. These policies aim to identify and assess potential vulnerabilities and risks, develop prevention and mitigation strategies, and enhance the resilience of critical systems against various threats, including natural disasters, cyberattacks, and terrorism. These policies often involve collaboration between government agencies, private sector entities, and international partners to create a comprehensive approach to infrastructure protection.

International Infrastructure Protection Policies:

Given the global nature of many infrastructure systems, international cooperation is essential to address the challenges posed by potential threats. International organizations such as the United Nations, Interpol, and the World Bank have developed frameworks and initiatives to promote information sharing, capacity building, and best practices exchange among nations. These policies aim to foster collaboration and coordination between countries, enhancing the collective ability to respond to and recover from infrastructure attacks or disruptions.

Challenges and Emerging Trends:

Infrastructure protection policies face numerous challenges in the 21st century. Rapid technological advancements, such as the Internet of Things (IoT), bring both opportunities and risks. The growing interconnectivity of critical systems introduces new vulnerabilities that need to be addressed. Additionally, the emergence of non-state actors as potential threats further complicates the landscape of infrastructure protection.

To address these challenges, policymakers need to stay vigilant and adapt their policies to the evolving threat landscape. This requires a multidisciplinary approach, involving experts in cybersecurity, engineering, and policy development. Furthermore, policies should be flexible enough to accommodate emerging technologies and rapidly changing threats.

Conclusion:

National and international infrastructure protection policies are vital in safeguarding critical systems against attacks and disruptions. Governments, private sector entities, and international organizations must work together to develop comprehensive strategies that enhance the resilience of infrastructure systems. By addressing challenges, staying informed about emerging trends, and fostering international cooperation, we can ensure the security and reliability of critical infrastructure in the 21st century. This subchapter provides an overview of the current state of infrastructure protection policies and highlights the importance of their continuous development and adaptation to keep pace with the ever-changing threat landscape.

Regulatory Frameworks for Critical Infrastructure Resilience

Introduction:

In an increasingly interconnected world, safeguarding critical infrastructure has become a paramount concern for governments, businesses, and individuals alike. The reliance on energy facilities, communication networks, and water treatment plants necessitates the development of robust regulatory frameworks to ensure their resilience against potential attacks and disruptions. This subchapter aims to explore the various regulatory approaches that can enhance the protection of critical infrastructure, thereby securing the functioning of societies and economies.

Understanding the Threat Landscape:

Before delving into regulatory frameworks, it is crucial to comprehend the evolving threat landscape. Rapid technological advancements and the rise of cyber warfare have opened up new avenues for potential attacks on critical infrastructure. State-sponsored hackers, terrorist organizations, and criminal syndicates are constantly seeking vulnerabilities to exploit, posing significant risks to the smooth operation of vital systems. Recognizing these threats is the first step towards developing effective regulatory measures.

International Cooperation and Standards:

Given the global nature of critical infrastructure networks, international cooperation is vital to ensure comprehensive protection. Governments, organizations, and security analysts must collaborate to establish common standards and best practices. International bodies, such as the United Nations and Interpol, play a significant role in facilitating this cooperation and fostering the exchange of information and expertise.

National Legislation and Regulatory Agencies:

At the national level, governments must enact legislation and establish regulatory agencies dedicated to infrastructure protection. These agencies would be responsible for setting and enforcing standards, conducting audits and assessments, and coordinating response efforts in the event of an attack or disruption. Close collaboration between the public and private sectors is essential, as private companies often operate critical infrastructure. Robust regulatory frameworks should provide adequate incentives for compliance while ensuring the necessary checks and balances.

Public-Private Partnerships:

Engaging the private sector through public-private partnerships (PPPs) can be instrumental in enhancing critical infrastructure resilience. PPPs encourage information sharing, joint planning, and resource allocation between government entities and private companies. Incentives, such as tax breaks and liability protections, can be provided to encourage greater private sector involvement in infrastructure protection efforts.

Continuous Monitoring and Risk Assessment:

Regulatory frameworks must emphasize the importance of continuous monitoring and risk assessment. Regular audits and vulnerability assessments should be conducted to identify potential weak points and develop appropriate mitigation strategies. By staying proactive and responsive to emerging threats, critical infrastructure resilience can be significantly improved.

Conclusion:

The regulatory frameworks for critical infrastructure resilience serve as a fundamental pillar in safeguarding vital systems against attacks and disruptions. By fostering international cooperation, enacting national legislation, promoting public-private partnerships, and emphasizing continuous monitoring, governments and organizations can enhance the resilience of critical infrastructure networks. As professors, students, journalists, politicians, authors, and security analysts, it is our collective responsibility to understand, advocate for, and contribute to the development of effective regulatory frameworks that protect the infrastructure upon which our societies and economies depend.

Public-Private Partnerships in Infrastructure Security

In today's interconnected world, the security of critical infrastructure has become a pressing concern for governments, businesses, and citizens alike. Infrastructure systems such as energy facilities, communication networks, and water treatment plants are vital to the functioning of societies and economies. Any disruption or attack on these systems can have severe consequences, ranging from economic losses to endangering public safety.

To safeguard critical infrastructure in the 21st century, a collaborative approach is required. Public-private partnerships (PPPs) have emerged as an effective strategy for addressing the complex challenges associated with infrastructure security. This subchapter explores the role and significance of PPPs in ensuring the resilience of critical systems.

PPPs offer a unique framework that combines the expertise, resources, and capabilities of both the public and private sectors. Governments bring regulatory oversight, policy direction, and access to intelligence and law enforcement agencies. On the other hand, private companies contribute with their technological innovation, operational efficiency, and financial investments. This synergy enables a comprehensive and holistic approach to infrastructure security.

The success of PPPs in infrastructure protection lies in their ability to foster collaboration, information sharing, and joint decision-making. By establishing clear lines of communication and coordination, stakeholders can work together to identify vulnerabilities, develop risk management strategies, and implement effective security measures. This partnership approach ensures that expertise from various domains, including engineering, cybersecurity, and emergency response, is leveraged to enhance the resilience of critical infrastructure.

Moreover, PPPs provide a platform for innovation and research. Universities and research institutions play a crucial role in these partnerships, offering fresh perspectives, conducting cutting-edge research, and training the next generation of security analysts. By engaging with academia, PPPs can tap into the latest advancements in technology, threat intelligence, and best practices. This collaborative environment encourages continuous learning and adaptation in the face of evolving security challenges.

The importance of PPPs in infrastructure security cannot be overstated, particularly in a world where threats are becoming increasingly sophisticated and ubiquitous. Through these partnerships, governments and private sector entities can pool their resources, knowledge, and capabilities to develop resilient infrastructure systems that are able to withstand and recover from attacks and disruptions.

In conclusion, public-private partnerships are crucial for safeguarding critical infrastructure in the 21st century. By leveraging the strengths of both sectors, these partnerships foster collaboration, innovation, and resilience. Professors, students, journalists, politicians, authors, and security analysts must recognize the significance of PPPs in infrastructure protection and actively support their development and implementation. Only through these partnerships can we ensure the security and resilience of critical systems upon which our societies and economies depend.

Chapter 9: Case Studies in Infrastructure Protection

Successful Examples of Infrastructure Protection

In the face of evolving threats and increasing vulnerabilities, safeguarding critical infrastructure has become a paramount concern for governments, organizations, and societies worldwide. The need to ensure the resilience of essential systems, such as energy facilities, communication networks, and water treatment plants, against attacks and disruptions has prompted innovative approaches to infrastructure protection. This subchapter explores several successful examples that exemplify the effectiveness of different strategies and technologies in securing critical infrastructure.

One notable success story is the implementation of advanced surveillance systems in major cities. By deploying state-of-the-art cameras, sensors, and analytics software, law enforcement agencies have significantly enhanced their ability to detect and prevent potential threats. For instance, London's extensive network of surveillance cameras played a crucial role in thwarting terrorist attacks during the 2012 Summer Olympics. The integration of these technologies with intelligent software algorithms enables real-time threat identification, enabling authorities to respond swiftly and effectively.

Another successful example lies in the realm of energy infrastructure protection. The United States' Strategic Petroleum Reserve (SPR) serves as a prime illustration of a robust defense against disruptions in the oil supply chain. With a network of underground storage facilities and a dedicated response team, the SPR has proven instrumental in mitigating the impact of natural disasters, geopolitical conflicts, and other crises on energy markets. This strategic approach has helped maintain stability in oil prices and ensured the nation's energy security.

Additionally, the advent of advanced cybersecurity measures has fortified the protection of critical communication networks. Governments and organizations have recognized the importance of securing these networks against cyber threats, which have the potential to cause significant disruptions. The establishment of dedicated cyber defense units, implementation of encryption technologies, and continuous monitoring of network traffic have proven effective in safeguarding critical information infrastructure.

Water treatment plants, too, have seen successful protection measures. The creation of redundancy systems and backup facilities has allowed for the uninterrupted supply of safe drinking water, even in the face of natural disasters or deliberate attacks. Furthermore, the implementation of water quality monitoring systems ensures early detection of contamination, enabling prompt response and preventing harm to public health.

These examples highlight the successful application of various strategies and technologies in safeguarding critical infrastructure. By studying these cases, professors, students, journalists, politicians, authors, and security analysts can gain valuable insights into the best practices and innovative solutions that can be employed to enhance the resilience of critical systems in the 21st century. With continued collaboration and investment in infrastructure protection, societies can better prepare for emerging threats and ensure the uninterrupted functioning of essential services that underpin our modern way of life.

Lessons Learned from Infrastructure Attacks and Disruptions

In today's interconnected world, the safety and resilience of critical infrastructure systems are paramount. From energy facilities and communication networks to water treatment plants, the protection of these crucial systems is essential for the smooth functioning of our societies. However, history has shown us that infrastructure is not immune to attacks and disruptions, and there are valuable lessons to be learned from past incidents.

This chapter aims to highlight some of the most significant lessons we have learned from infrastructure attacks and disruptions, providing valuable insights for professors, students, journalists, politicians, authors, and security analysts. By understanding these lessons, we can collectively work towards safeguarding critical systems in the 21st century.

Lesson 1: The evolving threat landscape - Infrastructure attacks and disruptions are no longer confined to physical acts of sabotage. Cyber threats have become increasingly sophisticated, and hackers are constantly finding new ways to exploit vulnerabilities in networked systems. It is crucial to recognize the ever-evolving nature of the threat landscape and develop robust defense strategies accordingly.

Lesson 2: Interdependency and cascading effects - Infrastructure systems are highly interconnected, and disruptions in one sector can have cascading effects on others. The 2003 Northeast blackout in the United States serves as a prime example, where a single tree falling on a power line led to a widespread outage affecting millions of people. Understanding interdependencies between critical systems is crucial for effective response and recovery.

Lesson 3: Importance of redundancy and resilience - Building redundancy and resilience into critical infrastructure is essential. Redundancy ensures that there are backup systems and alternate routes in place to mitigate the impact of disruptions. Resilience enables systems to withstand and recover quickly from attacks or disruptions. Investing in redundancy and resilience is a proactive approach towards protecting critical infrastructure.

Lesson 4: Collaboration and information sharing - Effective infrastructure protection requires collaboration between various stakeholders. Governments, private industries, academia, and security agencies must work together to share information, best practices, and threat intelligence. By fostering collaboration, we can enhance our collective ability to detect, prevent, and respond to attacks.

Lesson 5: Continuous monitoring and proactive defense - Infrastructure protection is not a one-time effort but a continuous process. Regular monitoring, threat assessments, and vulnerability testing are essential to identify and address potential weaknesses. Proactive defense measures, such as intrusion detection systems and incident response plans, are crucial to swiftly respond to attacks and minimize their impact.

In conclusion, the lessons learned from past infrastructure attacks and disruptions provide invaluable insights into safeguarding critical systems in the 21st century. By understanding the evolving threat landscape, recognizing interdependencies, investing in redundancy and resilience, fostering collaboration, and implementing continuous monitoring and proactive defense measures, we can collectively work towards a more secure and resilient infrastructure. This knowledge is essential for professors, students, journalists, politicians, authors, and security analysts involved in infrastructure protection, enabling them to make informed decisions and contribute to the safety of our critical systems.

Future Trends and Innovations in Infrastructure Security

As we move further into the 21st century, the importance of safeguarding critical infrastructure has become more apparent than ever before. With the increasing interconnectedness of our society and the growing reliance on technology, infrastructure protection has emerged as a pressing concern for governments, businesses, and individuals alike. In this subchapter, we will explore the future trends and innovations in infrastructure security that will shape the way we protect our critical systems.

One of the key trends in infrastructure security is the integration of advanced technologies such as artificial intelligence (AI) and machine learning. These technologies have the potential to revolutionize the way we detect and prevent attacks on critical infrastructure. By analyzing massive amounts of data in real-time, AI algorithms can identify anomalies and patterns that might indicate a security breach. This can enable security analysts to respond swiftly and effectively to potential threats, reducing the risk of disruptions.

Another important trend is the increasing adoption of decentralized and distributed systems. Traditional centralized systems are more vulnerable to attacks as they offer a single point of failure. In contrast, decentralized systems distribute critical functions across multiple nodes, making it harder for attackers to compromise the entire system. Blockchain technology, which underpins cryptocurrencies, holds promise in this regard by providing a secure and tamper-proof framework for managing and verifying transactions.

The Internet of Things (IoT) is also set to play a significant role in infrastructure security. As more devices become interconnected, the potential attack surface expands exponentially. However, IoT devices can also be leveraged to enhance security. For example, smart sensors and actuators can monitor and regulate access to critical infrastructure, detect physical threats, and initiate automated responses to mitigate risks.

Additionally, the convergence of physical and cybersecurity is expected to shape the future of infrastructure protection. Traditionally, physical security and cybersecurity have been treated as separate domains. However, as the lines between the physical and digital worlds blur, an integrated approach that combines both aspects is becoming essential. This includes technologies such as biometric authentication, video analytics, and advanced access control systems that bridge the gap between physical and digital security.

In conclusion, the future of infrastructure security is marked by the integration of advanced technologies, the adoption of decentralized systems, the utilization of IoT devices, and the convergence of physical and cybersecurity. These trends and innovations hold great promise in safeguarding critical infrastructure against attacks and disruptions. As professors, students, journalists, politicians, authors, and security analysts, it is essential to stay informed about these developments and collaborate to ensure the resilience of our critical systems in the face of emerging threats. "Infrastructure Under Siege: Safeguarding Critical Systems in the 21st Century" serves as a comprehensive guide to understanding and navigating this evolving landscape.

Chapter 10: The Way Forward

Recommendations for Enhancing Infrastructure Resilience

In today's interconnected world, the threats to critical infrastructure have become more prevalent and sophisticated than ever before. To safeguard our vital systems and ensure their resilience against attacks and disruptions, it is imperative that we take proactive measures to enhance infrastructure protection. This subchapter provides a comprehensive set of recommendations for various stakeholders, including professors, students, journalists, politicians, authors, and security analysts, who are invested in infrastructure resilience.

1. Education and Awareness:

Professors and students should collaborate to develop comprehensive courses and research programs focused on infrastructure protection. By raising awareness and understanding of the challenges faced in safeguarding critical systems, we can foster a new generation of experts in this field.

2. Public-Private Partnerships:

Journalists can play a crucial role in highlighting the importance of public-private partnerships in infrastructure resilience. They should actively report on successful collaborations between government agencies, private organizations, and academia, showcasing best practices and encouraging further cooperation.

3. Legislative Initiatives:

Politicians have a responsibility to enact legislation that promotes infrastructure resilience. They should work towards establishing robust regulatory frameworks, providing funding for research and development, and incentivizing private sector investment in protective measures.

4. Knowledge Sharing:

Authors can contribute by writing books, articles, and studies that disseminate knowledge on infrastructure protection. By sharing insights and lessons learned from previous incidents and successful mitigation strategies, they can help bridge the gap between theory and practice.

5. Threat Assessments:

Security analysts must conduct regular and thorough threat assessments to identify vulnerabilities and potential attack vectors. By staying ahead of emerging threats, they can provide valuable information to policymakers and infrastructure operators, enabling them to implement targeted protective measures.

6. Technological Innovation:

Professors, students, and researchers should focus on developing cutting-edge technologies to enhance infrastructure resilience. This includes advanced monitoring systems, secure communication networks, and robust physical protection measures to deter and mitigate attacks.

7. Resilience Exercises:

Infrastructure operators should regularly conduct resilience exercises to test their response capabilities and identify areas for improvement. These exercises should simulate various scenarios, including cyber-attacks, natural disasters, and physical intrusions, to ensure preparedness and enhance coordination among stakeholders.

By implementing these recommendations, we can collectively strengthen our critical systems and protect them from potential threats. The safeguarding of energy facilities, communication networks, and water treatment plants is not an individual effort but a shared responsibility. The collaboration between academia, government agencies, private organizations, and the media is crucial for achieving infrastructure resilience in the 21st century. Together, we can build a future where critical infrastructure remains secure and reliable, even in the face of evolving challenges.

Building Awareness and Collaboration for Critical Infrastructure Protection

In today's interconnected world, safeguarding critical infrastructure has become more vital than ever before. The protection of energy facilities, communication networks, and water treatment plants is paramount to ensuring the resilience of our societies against potential attacks and disruptions. This subchapter aims to address the importance of building awareness and collaboration in the field of critical infrastructure protection.

As professors, students, journalists, politicians, authors, and security analysts, you all play a crucial role in shaping public opinion, policy-making, and security measures. By understanding the challenges and risks faced by critical infrastructure, you can contribute to raising awareness among the general public and decision-makers alike.

Firstly, it is essential to comprehend the vulnerabilities present in our critical infrastructure. Through research and analysis, professors, students, and security analysts can identify potential weaknesses and propose innovative solutions. By disseminating this knowledge through academic papers, media articles, and reports, journalists and authors can help educate the public and decision-makers about the risks and the urgency to act.

Collaboration is another key aspect of protecting critical infrastructure. No single entity or sector can tackle this issue alone. Politicians must recognize the importance of cross-sector collaboration and create frameworks that encourage information sharing, coordination, and joint exercises. By bringing together experts from various fields, we can foster a holistic approach to infrastructure protection.

Furthermore, collaboration should extend beyond national borders. In an interconnected world, a cyber-attack on critical infrastructure in one country can have far-reaching consequences. Therefore, international cooperation is crucial. Policymakers must engage in diplomatic efforts to establish agreements for sharing threat intelligence, best practices, and joint response mechanisms. This cooperation can help build a robust defense against potential threats.

Finally, education and training programs should be developed to equip future professionals with the skills needed to protect critical infrastructure. Professors can incorporate this topic into their curricula, ensuring that students gain a comprehensive understanding of the challenges and solutions. Additionally, politicians can allocate resources to provide specialized training for security personnel responsible for critical infrastructure protection.

In conclusion, building awareness and collaboration is vital to safeguarding critical infrastructure in the 21st century. Professors, students, journalists, politicians, authors, and security analysts all have an important role in this endeavor. By understanding vulnerabilities, raising awareness, fostering collaboration, and investing in education and training, we can work towards ensuring the resilience and security of our critical systems. Together, we can protect our societies against potential threats and disruptions, ensuring a safer future for all.

The Role of Academia, Media, and Government in Safeguarding Critical Systems

In today's interconnected and rapidly evolving world, safeguarding critical systems has become a paramount concern. The protection of infrastructure, including energy facilities, communication networks, and water treatment plants, is crucial to ensure their resilience against attacks and disruptions. This subchapter explores the vital role that academia, media, and government play in this process.

Academia, as a center for research and knowledge, holds immense potential in safeguarding critical systems. Professors and students can engage in cutting-edge research to identify vulnerabilities and develop innovative solutions. By collaborating with industry experts and government agencies, academia can contribute to the development of robust technologies, protocols, and policies. Additionally, educational institutions can offer specialized programs and courses to train future professionals in infrastructure protection, fostering a skilled workforce that can address emerging challenges effectively.

Media, as a powerful communication tool, plays a crucial role in raising awareness and disseminating information about the vulnerabilities and risks faced by critical systems. Journalists can investigate and report on potential threats, as well as highlight successful strategies and best practices in infrastructure protection. By providing accurate and timely information to the public, the media can encourage individuals to take an active role in safeguarding critical systems, creating a culture of resilience and preparedness.

Government, as the primary custodian of public safety and security, has a critical responsibility to safeguard critical systems. Policymakers and politicians must enact legislation and regulations that promote a comprehensive and integrated approach to infrastructure protection. By establishing partnerships with academia and industry stakeholders, the government can facilitate research, innovation, and knowledge sharing. Moreover, government agencies should collaborate with international counterparts to address the global nature of threats to critical systems, ensuring effective coordination and response.

For all stakeholders involved, collaboration and information sharing are fundamental. Professors, students, journalists, politicians, authors, and security analysts must work together to exchange knowledge, insights, and experiences. This can be achieved through conferences, workshops, and forums where experts from different domains can collaborate, identify emerging threats, and devise strategies to mitigate risks. Such collaborative efforts will enhance the collective understanding of infrastructure protection and foster a multidisciplinary approach to safeguarding critical systems.

In conclusion, the role of academia, media, and government in safeguarding critical systems is indispensable. Through research, education, awareness, legislation, and collaboration, these stakeholders can contribute to the resilience, security, and sustainability of critical infrastructure. By working together, professors, students, journalists, politicians, authors, and security analysts can address the emerging challenges of the 21st century and ensure the protection of critical systems for future generations.

Conclusion: Safeguarding Critical Systems in the 21st Century

In today's interconnected world, safeguarding critical systems has become paramount to ensure the stability and resilience of our infrastructure. This subchapter delves into the importance of protecting crucial systems such as energy facilities, communication networks, and water treatment plants in the 21st century. Addressing an audience of professors, students, journalists, politicians, authors, and security analysts, it aims to highlight the significance of infrastructure protection and the challenges we face in securing these vital components of our society.

As our reliance on technology and interconnectedness grows, so does the potential for disruptive attacks on critical infrastructure. The digital age has brought immense benefits, but it has also exposed vulnerabilities that can be exploited by malicious actors. The increasing frequency and sophistication of cyber-attacks have demonstrated the urgent need for robust safeguards to protect our critical systems.

This subchapter explores the various strategies and approaches that can be employed to safeguard critical infrastructure. It emphasizes the importance of collaboration and coordination among stakeholders, including government agencies, private sector entities, and research institutions. Only through a collective effort can we effectively mitigate risks and build resilience in the face of emerging threats.

The subchapter also highlights the role of advanced technologies in infrastructure protection. From artificial intelligence and machine learning to blockchain and quantum computing, innovative solutions can enhance our ability to detect, prevent, and respond to attacks. However, these technologies must be deployed strategically, considering the potential risks and ethical implications they may bring.

Furthermore, the subchapter sheds light on the need for continuous investment in research and development to stay ahead of evolving threats. It emphasizes the importance of training and education in equipping professionals with the necessary skills to address the complex challenges in infrastructure protection.

Finally, the subchapter concludes by reinforcing the urgency of safeguarding critical systems in the 21st century. It stresses the importance of proactive measures, such as conducting thorough risk assessments, establishing robust incident response plans, and fostering international cooperation to combat global threats.

Overall, this subchapter serves as a call to action for all stakeholders involved in infrastructure protection. It seeks to raise awareness and inspire collaboration in safeguarding critical systems, ensuring their resilience against attacks and disruptions. By working together and staying vigilant, we can build a safer and more secure future for our critical infrastructure in the 21st century.

www.ingramcontent.com/pod-product-compliance
Lightning Source LLC
Chambersburg PA
CBHW031426160726
47993CB00003B/1419